Gordon Grant

SKETCHBOOK

Gordon Grant
by his friend
Oberhardt

Gordon Grant
SKETCHBOOK

PREFACE BY
Wade Hampton de Fontaine

INTRODUCTION BY
Norman Kent

WATSON-GUPTILL PUBLICATIONS
NEW YORK

PREFACE

A good many years have passed since I had the good fortune to meet Gordon Grant. My first contacts with him on a professional level were in my capacity as art director of Yachting magazine. Even though I had long been an admirer of his work, particularly his character studies, I had hesitated to approach so famous an artist because the art budget of the magazine was strictly limited. However, I finally decided I had nothing to lose, and, taking my courage in both hands, I called on the artist, fully expecting a polite refusal to the modest commission I had to offer. To my delight, not only was his reception cordial, but he also agreed to make the illustrations I wanted.

Over the years our acquaintance ripened into a friendship that has been immeasurably rewarding. The warmth and generosity of Mr. Grant's personality and the kindness with which he helped me with my own artistic efforts eventually lead to my vacationing at Rocky Neck in Gloucester, Massachusetts, where, for many years, he had a summer studio. Here we went on many sketching jaunts together; and it was during these outings that I came to know him well and to learn, from observation, many of his personal methods of drawing and painting.

Mr. Grant's sketching equipment was always unbelievably simple: a sketch pad of smooth paper with a spring clip to hold the pages when the breezes blew, a lead holder in which a Negro lead (either black or brown) was inserted, a pen knife, and a backless stool. That is all—no eraser, no stumps, no umbrella. But the sketches that were produced from these few materials were magic to behold. With a single pencil he could get every tone he wanted, from the most delicate gray to the darkest dark.

It was fascinating to watch him when we arrived at a chosen spot. He would wander around, sizing up the situation from many angles. He never just sat down and began sketching at once. After a subject was finally chosen, the things he could do with it were amazing. He tells the story of sketching at Ogunquit one day when a woman came along and glanced over his shoulder. She looked at the sketch and then at the scene and exclaimed, "But Mr. Grant, I don't see that big rock." He pointed out to her a stone perhaps a foot or so across. Its shape had interested him; so he had enlarged it to the size of a boulder to make his composition more interesting.

In Gordon Grant's work composition always comes first; details and reality are secondary. He tells another story which illustrates the point. One day a visitor who was staying at the same inn at Rocky Neck came to his studio to buy a watercolor. After much deliberation she selected a picture. Then she asked the locale of the subject. To her chagrin it turned out to be nowhere in particular. Gordon explained that painters, like composers, often improvise. He pointed out that a composer may choose a chord here, a run there and end up with a pleasing result, and that an artist is justified in following the same practice. In the painting in question his sketches had provided a group of houses from Rockport, a tree from Lanesville, a road from another part of Cape Ann; and the figures were created from whole cloth drawn from the inexhaustable storehouse of his memory and experience. The final result was a delightful picture, more truly representative of the spirit of Cape Ann than any painting made from a single subject could hope to be. His explanation finally convinced the buyer; she wrote out a check and went off happily with the watercolor, which, I was told later on, became her favorite painting.

I recall a certain day when, following Gordon down an overgrown lane and climbing over a couple of fences, we came to the sea. It was a spot he knew well; I think he knew every sketchable spot on Cape Ann. After the usual reconnoitering we settled down on the rocks—it was too rough for stools—and began our sketches. The scene was made up of a narrow foreshore strewn with small boulders, a low vertical rock fall to the left, and a rather large boulder—perhaps three feet in diameter—to the right. The water beyond was framed by the rocks. Actually, it didn't appeal to me as much of a subject, but I set to work to do the best I could. When my sketch was completed, I went over to see what Gordon had done. The small rock on the left had become a precipice about fifteen feet high and the three foot rock on the right a huge boulder. Between them the sea broke on the rocks with a fine show of flying spray. A dramatic composition had been created from a commonplace situation. This lesson made my second sketch quite different from my first one!

On another occasion we had gone to Lanesville, one of Cape Ann's most picturesque spots. Gordon settled down to pencil sketching and I began a watercolor. He finished first and came over to see what I had done. Just as he was looking at my finished sketch of the little harbor with its granite breakwaters and moored boats, a lobsterman came in and moored in the middle of the cove. I said that I was sorry the boat hadn't been there when I started my sketch. "Well," said he, "why don't you put it in now?" I turned to him and said, "How about your doing it?" To my delight he sat down and proceeded, with a few deft strokes, to put in the newcomer just where it did the most for the picture. Not only that, but he added touches here and there which pulled the whole thing together and gave my sketch a finish it had lacked. This watercolor is now one of my prized possessions.

Gordon's pencil sketching was only preliminary to the making of a finished watercolor in his studio. The morning after our Lanesville trip I went over to the studio to watch him convert his sketch of the day before. He selected a half sheet of 140-pound cold-pressed Whatman paper, which he had stretched, slightly damp, on his drawing board, fastening it all around with paper tape. When I arrived he had already sketched lightly in pencil the general outlines of the picture and was ready to proceed with his painting. He always stood to paint, keeping his board at a convenient height on a special drawing table slightly tilted before him. His paints, brushes, mixing trays, and water were on another table alongside. First he painted in the sky with a big flat brush, using an enamelled tray reserved for skys for a palette— keeping his colors clean and free of any contamination from unsuitable pigments. This went quickly, but I was interested to watch the care with which he applied his colors. He would set down a wash and wait for it to dry to just the degree he regarded as suitable before applying the next. He tested its moisture with the side of his hand from time to time until he felt it was ready for the next step.

The sky done, he put aside the mixing tray and carried on with his watercolor box. The picture came alive under his brush and was finished in a couple of hours. At his annual show at the Grand Central Gallery in New York that fall, I was pleased to see the picture I had watched from its inception with a red star affixed indicating it had been sold.

I like to look back on a particular summer night when the Grants joined my wife and me for dinner on the terrace of a waterside restaurant. After a pleasant meal, we adjourned to a gallery alongside Gordon's studio overlooking the harbor. Here we sat for a couple of hours in the warm night, watching the harbor lights, the stars, and the reflections of anchored boats in the dark water and listened to the Grants tell of their fifty years together. Gordon recalled as a boy sailing from San Francisco around Cape Horn in a square rigger when his father, a Scot by birth, had put him in the care of the ship's captain to be taken to Scotland to complete his schooling; and his experiences as a young newspaper artist on the San Francisco Examiner, before the turn of the century, and later on as a combat artist in the Boer War where Winston Churchill also served as correspondent for a London paper.

But best of all was the wonderful time when the Grants went together to France, where Gordon had revelled in making sketches and watercolors on the Normandy coast. Some of the drawings are to be found in this book. They hired a French driver who took them over the countryside to the Riviera and into Italy. The reminiscences were enlivened by recollections of picnics by the roadside and meals in country inns. What pleasant experiences to have stored away in one's memory.

Although Gordon Grant can paint a still life with the best of them and is a past master of characterization—particularly of waterfront seagoing types—he is probably best known for his wonderful sailing ships and his waterfront scenes. He loves the sea and always lived near it. His Gloucester studio literally overhung the water, and the inn where he and Mrs. Grant always stayed commands a fine view down the harbor. Fishing boats are always coming in and going out to sea, and yachts lie at anchor behind the big granite breakwater at Eastern Point.

He comes honestly by this love, since he was exposed to the sea, as few men are, from early youth. I have already mentioned his passage around Cape Horn in a sailing ship when still a boy. In later years he made a cruise to Alaska in one of the square riggers of the famous salmon packer fleet, and it was on that cruise that he made many of the sketches in this book.

Like most artists, Gordon Grant has great manual dexterity. The models of sailing ships and whaleboats that he has built are so beautifully constructed and finished that they are treasured collector's items.

Being of Scottish ancestry, Gordon Grant has a most practical outlook on life. As his fame as a marine artist became established, many commissions for advertising art were offered. He tells a story about a call he made on the art director of an advertising agency. He had been asked over to discuss a painting for an ad and on the way pondered what he should ask for the job. His mind ran to $500, but when the meeting was over and he was about to leave, the art director said: "Mr. Grant, I'm sorry but we have a limited budget for this account and all we can afford is $1500; I hope that will be all right with you." Gordon, the canny Scot, without batting an eye, replied that if that was their limit he would be glad to accept it!

Gordon Grant has received many honors in his long career as an artist. He is a National Academician and a member of many artists' clubs and societies. His paintings hang in The White House, the Library of Congress, and the Metropolitan Museum as well as many other museums and innumerable private collections. Probably his best known painting is *Old Ironsides,* thousands of reproductions of which were sold to raise funds for reconstructing the U. S. S. Constitution.

Over the years Gordon Grant has illustrated a great many books, and he has written and illustrated at least five: *Sail Ho!, Greasy Luck, Ships Under Sail, The Book of Old Ships,* and *Forty Famous Ships.* Every one of these has the tang of the salt sea wind clinging to it. Many of these illustrations are represented by his preliminary drawings and studies in this collection.

July 1960   WADE HAMPTON DE FONTAINE

INTRODUCTION

Shortly after my arrival in New York in 1943 to begin my first association with the present publisher, I was introduced to Gordon Grant. Like most artists of my generation, I had known his work for years—particularly his illustrated books, his etchings and lithographs —though my familiarity with his independent paintings in oil and watercolor was limited to an occasional reproduction in color in an art journal.

My first meeting with this artist, whose work I had genuinely admired, took place at the Salmagundi Club, that notable and venerable art institution on lower Fifth Avenue. It was a Friday evening in the late fall and I remember clearly that Gordon was seated at the central round table in the bar, surrounded by a group of convivial artists. His friends were interrogating him about his past summer in Rockport. He dismissed their inquiries about his paintings by saying that he had produced his usual bundle of drawings and watercolors for his annual fall show, and let it go at that. But then one of the artists asked Gordon to repeat one of his salty Scotch stories and the lid was off. Other members gathered around, for Gordon's fame as a raconteur was well known. The company included such admirable artists and illustrators as Edward A. Wilson, Walter Biggs, Stow Wengenroth, Ogden Pleissner and Harrison Cady—all Friday Night Regulars —and all among the many special friends of Gordon, then and now.

Like most men who have really accomplished something creditable in the art world, Gordon Grant's success has never unbalanced his innate modesty. Though, as I have stated, he is an engaging conversationalist, a storyteller and a natural mimic, who obviously enjoys holding forth among his confederates, he is equally contented as a good listener.

These characteristics of the man were borne out and amplified in successive years as I, too, became a part of the five-thirty circle that gathered on Fridays at Salmagundi and came to enjoy the flavor and friendship of this warm-hearted and handsome Scot. Beyond our frequent meetings at the club I have served on several juries with Gordon—experiences that only added to my appreciation of his artistic charity, always tempered by sound judgment.

But I have dwelt long enough on the personal. My commission is to write about Gordon Grant's drawings, or rather about his sketches — a term I am certain he would prefer us to use. For there is nothing pretentious or involved about these intimate notes, but rather a collection of sketches rapidly set down, in modest scale, with pencil or pen, and certainly with no idea of public scrutiny.

However, the publisher and editors are confident that this selection will find a receptive audience equally among those who know and admire Gordon Grant's paintings and among those who are devoted to the practice of the sketchbook habit.

Artists' sketchbooks generally fall into two classes. First, there are those that present orderly pages in which the draughtsman has obviously labored to produce rather complete statements; carefully wrought drawings, seldom fragmentary, and often carried out in full tonal range, whatever the medium. This is not to decry such miniature pictures, for to certain artists it is the only form of drawing that suits their temperament and direction.

It is the other kind that concerns us here, for Gordon Grant's sketchbooks are at opposite poles to the former. In his books one finds spontaneous sketches made under the prodding of immediacy: summary line used firmly and accented with rich blacks; studies for future reference that could and often have been incorporated into his painted compositions.

That the general subject matter of this artist's sketches concerns the sea, boats, and sailors is to be expected of a man who for fifty years has been dedicated to the tradition of sailing ships and whose paintings and illustrations have re-created an era that, like the steam locomotive, will soon become legendary.

Whenever artists discuss sailing ships they ultimately come to general agreement that Gordon Grant is one of a very few who has brought incontestable authority to his marine painting—authority born of intimate experience over a long period of time, reflected in a large body of work owned and cherished from coast to coast. It is safe to say that it is from such sketches as these, included in this selection, that Gordon has cemented his knowledge and gained the facility that is the style mark of his considerable accomplishment as an artist of distinction.

July 1960

NORMAN KENT
Editor, American Artist

Gordon Grant

SKETCHBOOK

Falmouth
Aug 11.

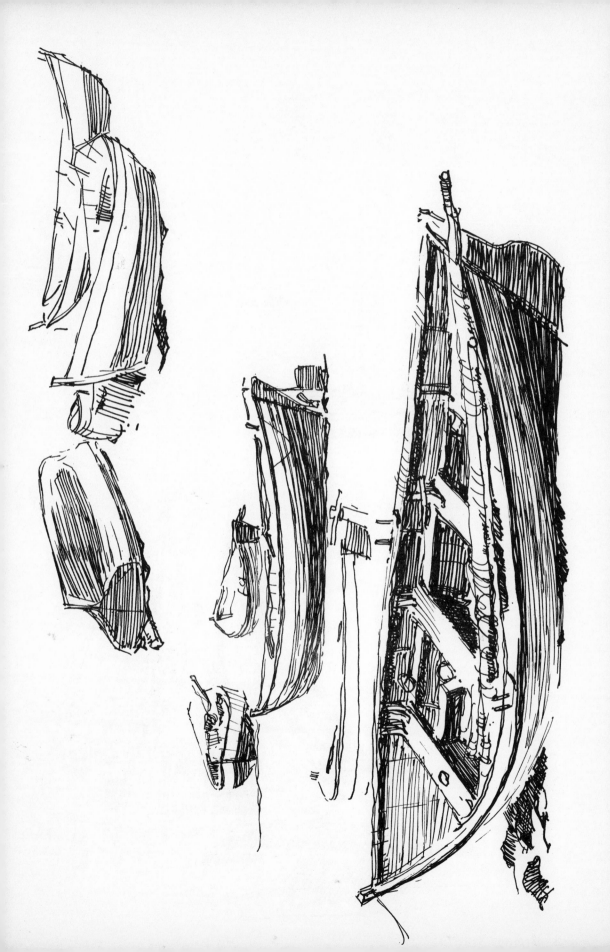

Rome -
June.

Marseilles

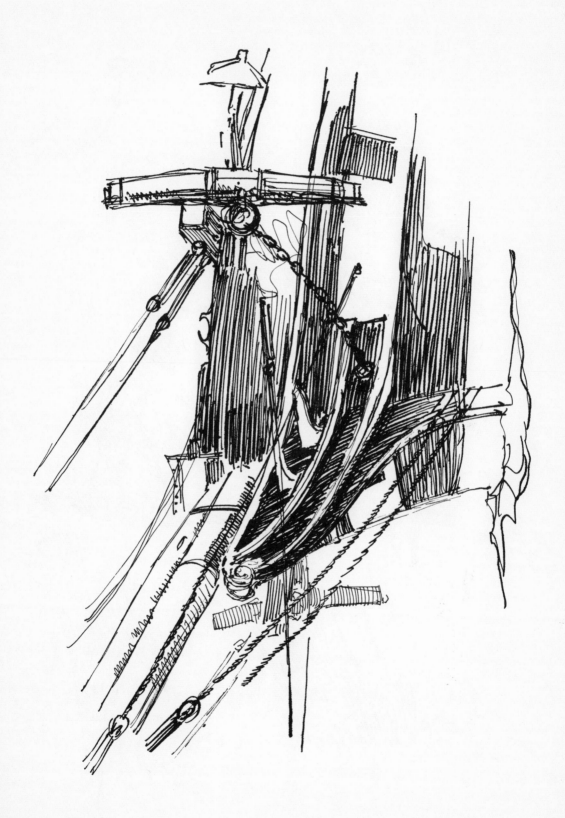

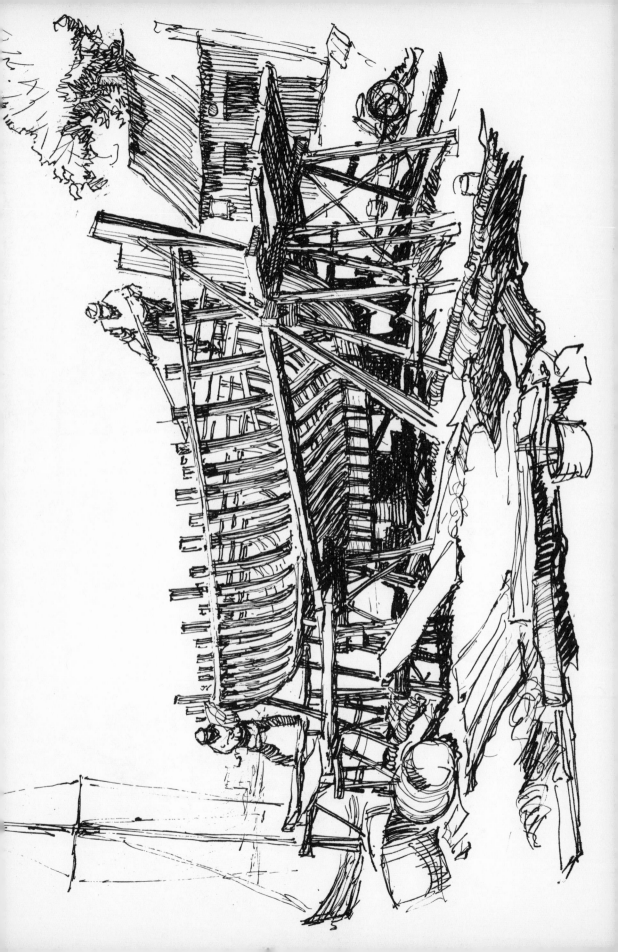

Naples.

Monte Cassino

Venice

New Bedford

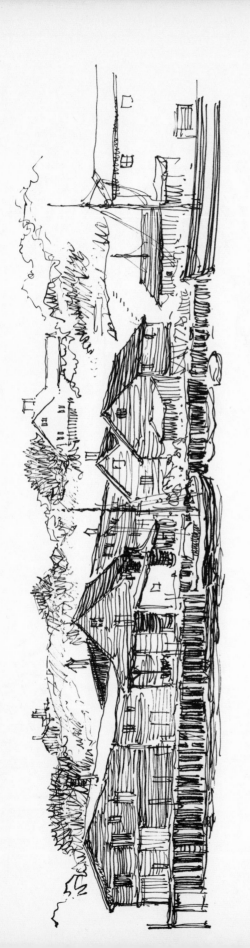

Concarneau

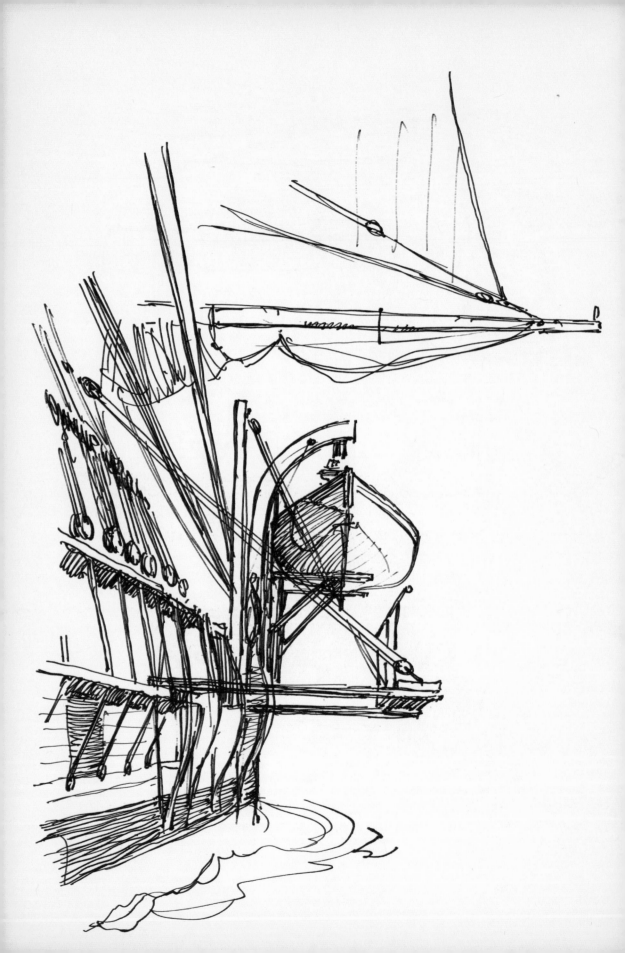

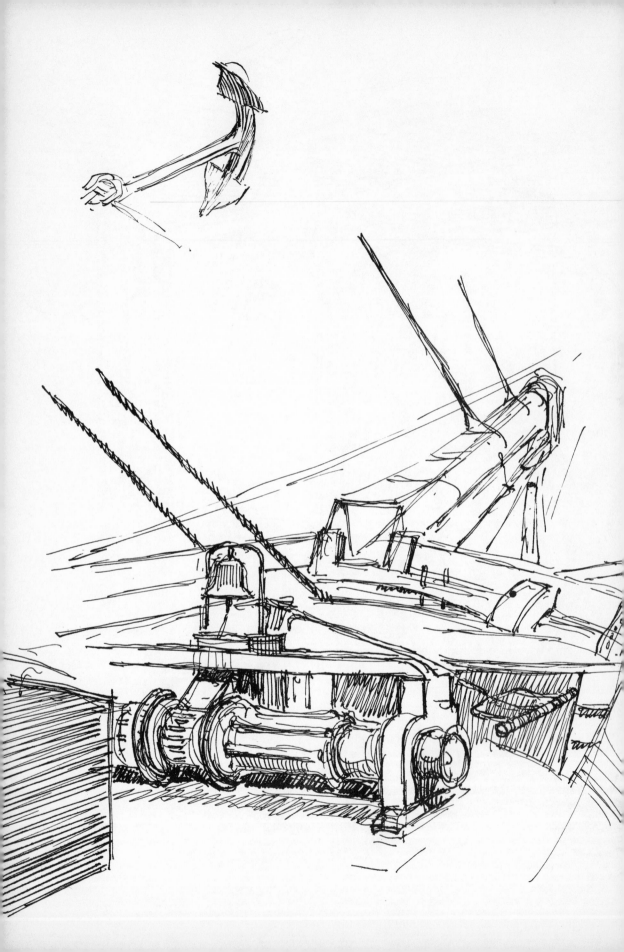

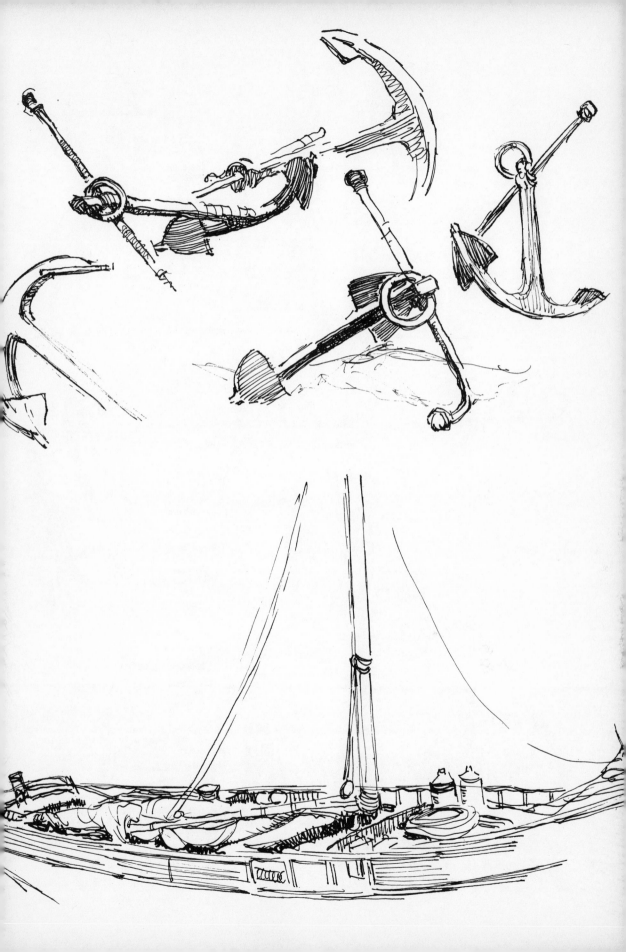

Falmouth